How to Overcome Envy and Jealousy

By Gerald Greene

Other Books by Gerald Greene

On the Brink – War with Iran Vol. 1 -4

Force Valor – Revenge

Love Lies Secrets

Gerald Greene Author Page

How to Overcome Envy and Jealousy. Copyright 2012. All rights reserved. No part of this book may be reproduced or transmitted in any form or by any means, electronic or mechanical including photocopying, recording, or by any information retrieval or system without express written permission from the publisher.

Table of Contents

By Gerald Greene

Chapter 1 – What is Envy?

Chapter 2 – What is Jealousy?

Chapter 3 – Jealous Behavior Reactions

Chapter 4 – Defending Against Jealousy

Chapter 5 - Why Are You Jealous?

Chapter 6 – Confront Your Feelings

Chapter 7 – Learning From Jealousy

Chapter 8 - Confidence in Yourself

Chapter 9 – Matt and Jane

Chapter 1 – What is Envy?

Envy is not the same as jealousy. The two emotions are often confused as they often are experienced by people who are insecure with their own accomplishments and sense of worth. Envy involves looking at the possessions, traits and lifestyle of others then comparing what that person has with yourself and your own situation. With envy you believe your own life is lacking and you deserve and should have whatever the other person has that you want.

When you are envious of others you are left feeling unhappy, resentful, angry, under-accomplished, inferior, underappreciated and discontented. All religions teach that envy is a sin as it interferes with the concern and love one should feel for their neighbors. Rather than love your neighbor you want things that your neighbor has and feel unhappy and resentful because you don't have them.

For example, let's say your next-door neighbor drives home in a brand new Mercedes GL-Class SUV. Rather than being pleased that your neighbor can enjoy such a fine automobile you become unhappy every time you see that undeserving son n' bitch pull in or out of his driveway behind the wheel of that status symbol. You become even unhappier when you get behind the wheel of your seven year old Chevrolet and begin your long, tiring, boring, commute to the office. Heck. You don't even have a GPS system in your car and your neighbor is driving around in a new Mercedes with all the bells and whistles. Fuck that bastard.

Once at your office the boss calls you from your cubicle to his exquisitely appointed corner office to ask when you will turn in the report you've been slaving away at for the past month. You look around at the boss's four hundred square foot office and compare it to your 32 square foot cubicle. If your boss is so smart why does he continue to ask such stupid questions about your report? The bastard doesn't deserve to have such a fine office. You should have his position and office and he should be the one in the tiny cubicle working on a report that will never be read.

Once again envy has raised its ugly head. Envy is brought on by feelings that others have more than you have, or have things you deserve but do not have. Envy is a dangerous emotion that brings on a state of unhappiness and discontent and can cloud judgment about your own worth and abilities. It is a natural human trait to occasionally desire things another person has. So you shouldn't beat yourself up if you are occasionally envious. However, to be constantly envious of your friends, coworkers, family, and acquaintances possessions or achievements, rather than being appreciative, is unhealthy and will lead to a great deal of unhappiness.

Chapter 2 – What is Jealousy?

Jealousy occurs when a person feels that an important relationship is intruded on and threatened by someone outside of the relationship. The relationship may be romantic, platonic, friendship, parent-child, sibling, boss, coach, or even an acquaintance that you hope to develop a closer relationship with. While jealousy is usually thought of as occurring in romantic situations it often occurs in the context of competitive situations, such as sports, family relationships (mother loves my sister more than me), the workplace, or education.

Jealousy is an all too common emotion. Most humans have experienced jealousy from time to time. The problem is that jealousy is usually confused as a sign of love, devotion, or deep caring for another person. Actually, the feeling of fear and apprehension that is typical of jealousy means that you don't feel secure in the relationship and wish to exercise control over your partner's activities. Being jealous means you lack trust in your partner or friend and fear you will lose him/her to another.

Being jealous is a form of being selfish. You want to have your partner or persons in an important relationship all to yourself and become apprehensive whenever they seem to show any interest at all in another person. Their interest may be completely plutonic. It may be that they are only being polite and acknowledging another person's presence. However, when you are jealous you still have the fear of losing the affection of your partner or person of interest.

Being overly jealous is a sure way to wreck a relationship. No one enjoys being constantly questioned about the places they have been, who they spoke with, why they will be later than usual in coming home after work, why they have the desire or need to be with anyone except you. In a romantic relationship should you constantly nag your partner about their every movement, conversation with another person, or glance at another human body, you will likely have a relationship headed for breakup. You may think your abusive, nagging actions are based upon love but in reality they are based upon fear.

If you don't feel safe and secure with your relationships you likely have some work to do in developing emotional maturity. It probably is your own confidence and emotional growth that needs bucking up. Unless you get a handle on jealousy and gain security with your relationship's status you will be unhappy and your relationship will suffer.

Again, it is important to distinguish between jealousy and love. If you truly love someone in a mature way you should not want to imprison, trap, or control them. If you want to have a long-term meaningful relationship you must trust them; give them their own space. If you are constantly jealous that is a sign of immaturity on your part. Jealousy can quickly pull your relationships apart. If it is a romantic relationship the thing you fear the most will likely happen. Your partner will tire of your frequent complaints and nagging and find a more mature person to build a relationship with.

Remember, having feelings of jealousy center on a fear of loss. The unpleasant feelings of fear, anger, and anxiety originate from a lack of trust. It is usually your own sense of insecurity that leads to a lack of trust.

Let's go through a couple of scenarios of jealousy interfering with what started out as a solid, caring, loving relationship.

Matt has been dating Jane for a year. Everything is great as long as Matt devotes 100% of his time to Jane. However, on the few occasions Matt had dinner and a few drinks with coworkers Jane became furious. Matt was not disrespectful; on each occasion he called Jane to let her know he would be coming home late and promised to be home by 10:30 PM. Unfortunately for their relationship each time he arrived home, even though he was never late, Jane began an interrogation.

"Did you enjoy your night out while I watched TV all by myself?"

"I had a nice time. The meal was really good."

"Who was there?" Jane's voice is a bit shrill and demanding.

"Only a few friends from the office. You know John, Bill, and Frank. And our new associate, Amy."

"What! You are out having dinner with a woman?"

"Not really. John, Bill, and Frank were there. We were all at the same table."

"What does she look like? Do you find her attractive?"

"She's not bad. But, Jane, I'm not interested in Amy. She's just someone I work with."

"Yeah, I bet. Did you sit next to her? Did you buy her drinks?"

And so it goes. On and on. Question after question. After a year of being a loyal faithful partner Matt is offended by the frequent questioning and begins to think something is wrong with his relationship. He increasingly finds the interrogations unpleasant and is beginning to feel trapped and closed in. It's a feeling that leads to frustration and unhappiness and the thought that he needs to seriously reconsider his relationship with Jane. Maybe he should see more of Amy after all.

Matt has his own relationship problems of jealousy interfering with Jane's happiness. Consider this scenario:

On the last Friday of every month Jane has a standing date with two former college classmate girlfriends. They meet at a popular neighborhood restaurant for dinner. After dinner they move to the lounge to listen to a popular local band and enjoy a couple of drinks before returning home. Jane always returns to the house before 11:00 PM. Jane really looks forward to the dinners as the girls exchange news, comment on each other's hairstyles and clothing, engage in a bit of gossip, and laugh a lot. They have a great time spending a few hours together.

Matt is very aware of this ritual dinner and at first quietly accepts the arrangement. However, one Friday evening Matt becomes suspicious as Jane returns home to change clothes before going to the restaurant. She puts on a new little black dress that Matt absolutely loves. Jane thought the dress was inappropriate for the office as it is too dressy and cut a little low in the front. Matt loves the modest amount of cleavage the dress reveals but is concerned Jane is wearing it without him being at her side. Matt makes the mistake of asking Jane why she is wearing that dress and was not satisfied with her answer that she only wants to show it to her girlfriends.

Jane's two girlfriends love the dress. Jane returns home by 11:00 PM in a great mood only to be greeted by a hostile Matt who has let his imagination go wild. He begins his own interrogation.

"Where were you tonight?"

"Matt honey, we ate where we always meet and eat. You know that Italian restaurant and lounge only three blocks from here on Second Avenue. "

"Who were you with? "

"You know I always meet Joanne and Nancy. They're my best girlfriends. You've met them both."

"Yeah, why did you dress up? And why did you show off your boobs?"

"Pardon me? What did you say?"

"You were showing off your boobs. I bet you found an admirer in the lounge. I bet he liked those boobs. Right?"

Uh oh. Matt's jealousy has unleashed a green eyed monster that is about to bring forth a raging demon lurking deep within Jane's petite body.

"Matt, you're crazy. I wanted to show off my new dress to my girlfriends, that's all. You're way out of line, Mister. Fuck you."

And with that Jane heads for the bedroom, slams and locks the door. Matt's jealousy over Jane's imagined male admirer has earned him a night sleeping on the couch. And Matt will have a guaranteed icy reception in the morning. Jane begins to think she might be better off living by herself.

In this example the emotion of jealousy is causing trouble even though the fear of loss is to an imaginary person. Even if the person were real he would be insignificant. Jane really is loyal to Matt and would not violate his trust. Even if she had spoken to another man she would have cut the conversation short if it turned sexual in nature.

Matt has a lot of work to do to gain the maturity that is required to have a successful long-term relationship. The problem is Matt blames Jane's harmless behavior for his feelings of frustration and anger and fails to understand that his excessive jealousy is undermining the relationship.

Chapter 3 – Jealous Behavior Reactions

You should take a hard look at the reaction and the effect your jealous suspicious mind has on your relationship with other people. This is especially important if your jealousy involves a lover or close friend. When you accuse someone of something they are innocent of you are sure to get a defensive reaction. An angry defensive action can quickly escalate into a relationship damaging event. You must be careful not to justify your jealously fueled accusations, and a partner or friends defensive reactions to those accusations, as confirmation of your suspicions.

Defensiveness is a natural response by people who are placed under pressure to justify their actions. If you constantly question your partner's whereabouts, dress, spoken words, and motives you are going to create some problems for the relationship. It doesn't take many occasions of nagging rounds of questioning to sour the relationship.

No one likes being constantly questioned as to what they're doing, where they're going, who they are seeing, and where they have been. That line of questioning is tiring, offensive, disparaging and quickly demoralizing. People who feel attacked, abused, and squeezed by a jealous line of questioning and assumptions will feel unhappy, undermined, badgered, frustrated and probably pissed off. Their natural reactions will soon display impatience, frustration, irritation and anger.

These emotions should not be taken as confirmations of guilt. They are signs that the person does not appreciate the hostile line of questioning and is defending his or her innocent nonthreatening actions. If you attack your friend or lover with an interrogation based on jealousy and decide that person is unwilling and incapable of fending off the advances of a new friend or would be lover, you have placed that person in a difficult, unfortunate position. One they are going to be very unhappy with.

They will likely try to reassure you that there is nothing threatening about their behavior and you have nothing to worry about. At the same time they will realize the lack of trust you have in them places a restraint and unsettling element of mistrust in the relationship; mistrust that previously wasn't there. Just place yourself into your lover or friend's position. How would you react if interrogated in an accusing, even hostile way? Can you see that a recurring pattern of jealous fueled interrogations will seriously damage, perhaps even end, what started out as a fun, loving and caring relationship?

If you wish for your relationship to continue you must learn to control your jealousy. You must trust your partner to abide by the constraints you have agreed should govern your relationship. If those constraints are unrealistic, say you have agreed that neither of you will even speak to another person, your relationship is likely doomed from the beginning. It is unrealistic and unwise to enter into such a confining agreement as it defies human nature.

A much more natural and realistic agreement would be that you agree that neither of you will sleep with another person while you are in your relationship. If that is your agreement you should trust the other person to abide by that agreement and not be jealous should that person occasionally wish to spend time with another person, even if that person is of the opposite gender. Trust must be an important part of any lasting relationship and is the best cure for control of jealousy. With complete trust there should be no fear you're in danger of losing the affection of your partner.

Chapter 4 – Defending Against Jealousy

Jealousy is a very common human emotion. Nearly all humans display the emotion of jealousy at some point in their lives. It is important to understand that jealousy is a combination of fear and anger and can be extremely destructive to relationships. Not only is it a destructive emotion it can be dangerous. So-called crimes of passion often occur because one partner is jealous of another partner's relationship with another person and loses control of their emotions. In an emotionally immature, jealous person fear and anger can turn into rage with disastrous results.

Your number one step in learning to overcome jealousy is to recognize when it occurs. Jealousy is fed by the fear of losing someone and anger that someone else is "moving in" and "taking away" a person or situation that you value and "belongs" to you. A frank self-analysis of your emotional maturity is required to understand and control jealousy.

If you think because you love someone you should control every aspect of their life you have a lot of work to do to gain emotional maturity. Few humans find everything they need in life in one other human being. The need to be social and to interact with a variety of humans is hardwired into most of us. Gaining this understanding of the social nature of nearly all humans will go a long way towards controlling jealousy.

Once you understand that it is only natural for your significant other to want to have some contact with other individuals you are on your way towards controlling jealousy. You must learn to be confident enough in the strength of your relationship to trust your partner to act appropriately when having contact with other people. If you can't trust your partner you won't be able to maintain a healthy relationship. An intimate relationship without trust will soon fail.

Being able to have sincere and direct communications with your partner is absolutely necessary in order to keep jealousy under control. If you are male and feel that it is important that you have your boys night out with your friends once or twice a month this should be communicated to your partner before entering into a couple's relationship. The same is true if you are a female who values time spent with your girlfriends or perhaps have male friends you would like to spend time with from time to time. Whatever needs are important to you should be conveyed to your partner or better yet, potential partner, to avoid feelings of jealousy and resentment that may come later if these discussions do not occur.

Feelings of jealousy may occur in various situations that are not at all romantic. For example, perhaps you are an athlete who is jealous because the head football coach considers you a second string quarterback. You are jealous of the young man who is the starting quarterback. It's your opinion that you deserve the starting position. Rather than strive to work harder to earn the position in your jealousy you become angry and resentful and lose focus and ease up on your workout routine. Once again jealousy proves to be a destructive emotion; one that demands emotional maturity to overcome.

Rather than become jealous a better course of action for the athlete would be to have a heart to heart talk with the coach, seek advice in the areas that need improvement to become a first string college quarterback, and then make a noticeable sincere effort to improve in those skill sets. While the athlete may not have the physical and mental skills necessary to become a starting quarterback this approach would likely improve his performance and certainly gain him the respect of the coach. It never hurts one to gain respect. Displaying jealous behavior is a sure way not to get it.

Jealousy among siblings is quite common. The competition between siblings for the affection of their parents can be quite intense and can adversely affect the relationships between the siblings. Once again in order to overcome jealousy a certain level of maturity must be obtained. A sibling experiencing the fear, anxiety, and apprehension that accompanies the emotion of jealousy must come to realize that each individual is different and that the level of attention given to each sibling will reflect that fact. It is only natural that the youngest less developed siblings receive the most attention as the youngest can do fewer things by themselves and require more assistance from parents. If one truly loves their siblings they should be pleased to see them receive the attention they require.

As siblings grow older a mature individual will realize sibling's accomplishments should be celebrated; not feared as something that will diminish their own relationship with their parents. For example, one of your siblings may develop skills as a wonderful concert pianist. This is an accomplishment that the entire family should be proud of. To be jealous of that sibling would be a terrible waste of energy and most counterproductive to a good relationship.

When the emotion of jealousy emerges it should immediately be confronted and identified for what it almost always is; a feeling of fear of loss without merit. Of course, your parents would be proud of your sibling's achievement as you should be. They will still love and respect you for your own achievements. There is no room for harboring jealousy in mature relationships. One should immediately recognize jealousy for what it is, thereby controlling the emotion before it has a chance to seriously damage your relationship.

It may be that your agreement with your partner is for you to have an open relationship. That is, you and your partner agree it is occasionally OK, and you have the other's permission, to spend time with, perhaps even be sexually involved, with another person so long as safe sex is observed. If that agreement is fully understood from the get go there should be no jealousy should your partner or you occasionally seek the company of another. You may even agree that group sex is acceptable. If so, that understanding should be agreed to well in advance of any group sexual activities and you should have an absolute feeling of trust that such activities will not damage your relationship. Obviously, if you are going to be jealous and fearful of each other's activities in any sexual encounters with other partners you should avoid such activities in the first place.

It is probably unwise to enter into an intimate relationship with someone you know to be intensely jealous. A person entering into an intimate relationship may at first accept the actions of a controlling jealous partner. That accepting person may think they can change their partner's behavior patterns. Changing the jealous emotions of another person is not impossible but is difficult as change must come through the efforts of the person whose behavior needs to be modified. That means the person must agree that their jealousy is a problem and must be willing to work at gaining maturity in order to correct the problem.

A person who is in a close relationship with an excessively jealous person will probably soon become weary of constant questioning and harassment about their activities. Someone who is extremely jealous will become angry and agitated if their partner even glances at another person. Being subject to such abuse is not pleasant for most individuals. They will likely begin to question the love and devotion they thought they had for a jealous partner long before their partner modifies his/her behavior. That is if he/her ever does.

Chapter 5 - Why Are You Jealous?

If you are the jealous type and sincerely wish to reign in the emotion you need to try and figure out why you're feeling jealous.

Extreme jealousy is often brought about by some experience in the past where the actions of a person you felt close to brought about a lack of trust. You still feel a sense of betrayal and find it difficult to now have a level of trust in another person. Even though conditions with your present partner may be far different, and hopefully greatly improved, you still fear that the breach of trust that occurred in the past will be repeated.

Additional factors in feeling jealous include anger toward yourself, feelings of insecurity, fear of being abandoned, and being vulnerable to the actions of someone you think you love or wish to be close to. The fear of loss is a powerful human trait that is a major component of jealousy.

You need to be honest with yourself and admit that you become jealous whenever you feel threatened and fear the person you wish to be with can't be trusted and may abandon you for another. Realistically, there may be no good reason to not trust the other person. If you find them chatting with someone you don't know they probably are just being polite and having a casual conversation with someone who has approached them. There usually is no good reason, no basis, for your lack of trust. It is unlikely they are thinking of leaving you. Unless your jealous bad behavior is driving them crazy.

You shouldn't beat yourself up too much because you have feelings of jealousy. Most people have jealous moments in life. However, you should work to bring your jealousy under control and can best accomplish this by staying objective about why you have such feelings. If you fear being abandoned by your partner you should sit down with that partner and let them know that is why you're so jealous. If you have a solid relationship and communicate honestly with each other you can develop a mutual trust that will take your relationship to a much higher level of development and maturity.

Let's once again check in with Jane and Matt and see if they have made progress in curbing Matt's feelings of jealousy. They are having dinner at their favorite Italian restaurant. It's the same restaurant Jane meets her girlfriends at once a month.

"No wonder you meet here with your girlfriends. The food is delicious. It's reasonably priced too."

"Yes, it's wonderful. I'm so glad you like it as much as I do."

Two couples enter the restaurant and are seated at the adjacent table. Jane suddenly exclaims in an excited voice, "Joanne! Nancy! What a pleasant surprise. Aren't you going to introduce us to those handsome gentleman you're with?"

Joanne quickly replies, "Jane, Matt. It's so good to see you. Matt and Jane this is Art Caliendo and Bert Fischer. Art and I went to high school together. Art and Bert work together."

After the usual greetings the new arrivals order a round of drinks and include Jane and Matt. They order their dinners. Jane and Matt continue with their meal. Matt notices that Bert keeps glancing at Jane who happens to be wearing her little black dress with the low-cut neckline. Finally, Bert leans towards Jane and asks, "You look familiar. Did you graduate from Princeton?"

"Why yes, I graduated in 2005. Did you go to Princeton?"

"Yes I did, class of 2004. I thought I recognized you. It's great to see you again."

Matt does not take part in the conversation or try in anyway to be friendly. In fact, his facial muscles tense and he doesn't try to hide the fact that he is becoming quite angry. The green eyed monster named Jealousy has taken full control of Matt's emotions. He is barely able to control himself until he is driving home and alone with Jane in the car.

"Why were you flirting with that guy? Does he turn you on?"

"Don't get started Matt. I was just trying to be polite. I didn't know Bart at college. I don't even remember him. He just happened to remember my face, that's all."

"Are you sure? He certainly seemed to be interested. He hardly paid any attention to Nancy."

"Matt you're imagining things. He was just being friendly. That's something you failed to do. You were actually hostile. It was embarrassing."

"I noticed the way you looked at him. Do you think I'm blind?"

Yikes! Another evening that started out pleasantly enough has turned sour. Our friend Matt has a lot of growing up to do if he wants to maintain a close relationship with Jane. Sure, Jane turns heads wherever she goes. She is an attractive woman with a pleasing personality. Matt must understand that while Jane receives a lot of attention she is a loyal and caring partner. But her patience is not infinite. Unless Matt overcomes his fear of loss and insecurity and learns to trust her he will lose Jane. No one enjoys being with a partner whose jealousy is completely without merit. Jane is not even flirting, just being polite to a girlfriend's date.

Chapter 6 – Confront Your Feelings

If you want to overcome jealousy you must learn to recognize and confront your feelings. As soon as jealousy emerges you need to ask yourself, *"Why am I getting angry and fearful? Why do I feel threatened? Who do I fear and why? Is there a genuine threat to my well-being? Why am I so tense? Is my partner really getting out of line or is my imagination getting the best of me?"*

These and similar questions should be asked to yourself as soon as you recognize the anger, fear, and frustration of jealousy. When you admit you are having feelings of jealousy you can isolate and identify them and bring your emotions under control. The ability to be honest with yourself and to directly confront your feelings goes a long way in gaining the understanding that jealousy is a destructive emotion that with some effort can be considerably diminished if not completely eliminated. The key is to confront your feelings as soon as they emerge.

Often it is false, baseless beliefs that underlie feelings of jealousy. By examining and confronting the beliefs you can eliminate the feelings of jealousy. A person who constantly has negative thoughts is usually an unhappy person who compounds that unhappiness by being jealous. If you believe that bad things always happen to you and constantly worry that yet another bad thing is about to happen you need to change your belief system.

You must ask yourself what possible benefit remaining negative will give you? Choosing to harbor false, baseless beliefs and remaining a negative person will ruin your relationships and poison your life. Beliefs are changeable by choice. When you examine and confront your beliefs you can change the way you feel. When you examine your fears and find them baseless you can decide to embrace positive thoughts. You will overcome jealousy as you become a positive thinking person.

The key is to embrace beliefs that are nurturing and supportive. Instead of thinking that your partner is going to leave you by your actions give them every reason to stay. Extend full support and loyalty to them and in every case if they are the right partner you will receive loyalty and support in return. Believe that the positive actions you take today will shape your future and pave the way towards a better life. When you become a positive person you will lose your fear of being abandoned and diminish, perhaps end, feelings of destructive jealousy.

When you realize being a negative person will adversely impact your entire life you will take steps to confront your false beliefs and take steps to create a happy and fulfilling life. Anger and fear will become far easier to manage. Once you reduce or remove the fuel for jealous feelings those unpleasant feelings will become controllable or not there at all.

Learning to control the emotion of jealousy is a process; it is unlikely you will be able to do it overnight. That means until you are able to bring your jealousy under control there will likely be incidents where your jealousy leads to comments and actions made to your partner you soon regret. Again, it is important to confront your feelings and to realize that most of them, perhaps all, are baseless, and your interrogation of your partner was rude and counterproductive.

If you have gone too far while under the influence of jealousy it is important that you apologize to your partner, the sooner the better. By not apologizing you are actually punishing your partner for your bad behavior. You should not make the act of apologizing lengthily or complicated. A simple "I'm really sorry I became so jealous and said such stupid things. I let my imagination run away with me. I'll try not to let it happen again." By apologizing you can begin repairing damage done by cruel and careless comments, accusations, and actions.

You should have a sincere conversation with your partner where you are open about your feelings of jealousy. You should examine your feelings of fear, apprehension, and anger. By confronting and discussing your feelings you are taking constructive actions that should help mend the damage done to the relationship by your accusations.

When discussing your feelings of jealousy with your partner you should take care that you accept responsibility for your actions. It would be a mistake to blame your partner for what you said or did. Be sure to listen to any comments your partner cares to make. Do not become defensive and interrupt should he/she say anything that you feel is in error. Remember there are always two sides to every story and your perception of what took place may be far different than your partner's perception.

You must acknowledge you realize your jealousy damages your relationship with your partner and causes harm. You must be passionate about their desire to overcome jealousy and be determined to overcome your immaturity. Make a clear statement to your partner that you will make every effort to outgrow jealousy.

You should acknowledge that eliminating feelings of jealousy is a process and that there could be other incidents where jealousy gets the best you. You need to agree to have other conversations with your partner if need be. Ask for their help as you continue to work on your jealousy problem and ask them to be frank in their comments. It is important not to beat yourself up too badly as you discuss what is after all a common human trait. Having compassion for yourself and for your partner is desirable as you seek to work together to find a better way forward.

Chapter 7 – Learning From Jealousy

Jealousy is an ignoble, negative, destructive, emotion that is present in most human beings. The emotion still has an important role in our lives as by working and struggling to overcome jealousy we can make ourselves better human beings who have a more positive outlook on life.

People often have a fear of loss when a relationship is new and the couple has not yet developed a full measure of trust. Both individuals likely have feelings of vulnerability as well as being overly possessive. These characteristics of a young relationship drive jealousy.

We can learn from jealousy as we seek to strengthen the relationship. By working to overcome jealousy we are working towards becoming better human beings and certainly better partners. The development of a caring and loving relationship with complete trust in the partner elevates the relationship to a level that is immensely satisfying. Once that level of personal development and maturity has been reached by both partners it is unlikely that jealousy will remain an issue. It will have served its purpose by motivating the partners to seek to eliminate the emotion before it causes irreparable damage to the relationship.

In a romantic relationship it is easy to become jealous because you feel your partner has a roving eye. Once again we can learn from jealousy. If we value the relationship jealousy should force us to examine the reasons why our partners, whether they are male or female, seem to be constantly checking out numbers of the opposite sex. A fair examination of the problem will determine that it isn't a problem at all. The roving eye is biologically driven and is completely natural for the human species.

In the vast majority of cases the fact your partner is checking out everyone within their sight doesn't mean they are planning to leave you. For most people it is only about appreciating and marveling over the human form and is not about looking for another more suitable partner. The tremendous variety of human shapes fascinates most people. Misunderstanding between couples as to why one or both of them are looking about at other human forms has created feelings of jealousy and created conflict between couples for as long as relationships have existed.

In a mature relationship the individuals will discuss their feelings and quickly decide that the fear of loss and apprehension about their partner's roving eye is completely unwarranted. Overcoming such feelings of jealousy becomes a learning experience; one that will encourage frank communications between partners and only strengthens the relationship.

Chapter 8 - Confidence in Yourself

One all the best ways to overcome envy and jealousy is to develop trust and confidence in yourself. Both envy and jealousy are ignoble emotions. Most humans develop early in life excessive amounts of both emotions. To have a better chance at a happy, fulfilling life you should strive to gain control over both envy and jealousy and reduce the accompanying feelings of fear, apprehension, foreboding, desire, and negativity to manageable levels. Ideally, one would completely cleanse the brain of these feelings.

To refresh the memory, envy involves looking at the possessions, traits or lifestyle of others then comparing what that person has with yourself and your own situation. You want to have for yourself what that person has but aren't necessarily willing to take the steps in put in the work necessary to obtain it. You just want it and you want it now.

Jealousy evolves more than anything around a fear of loss. You fear that something you value, a person, job, recognition, office, some form of status symbol, or anything you place a high value on, will go to someone else when you are the one who deserves it. All religions classify envy and jealousy as sins since the emotions interfere with a person's happiness and unchecked can cause harm to you as well as to other people. With envy you desire the property or traits of another and with jealousy you hurt yourself and others. Both emotions lead to destructive feelings and bad behavior.

When you have self- confidence you have a positive feeling about yourself. You have decided to eliminate negative thoughts and replace them with positive thoughts and feelings. This doesn't mean that you have become unrealistic; from time to time all of us have to deal with unpleasant aspects of life and unexpected events that can interfere with our normal routines. However, by being a positive person you will retain your equilibrium and find a way to solve any problems. If you are trapped in negativity you have a greatly reduced ability to solve problems and to lead a happy and productive life.

With self-confidence you are much less likely to remain jealous. You lose your fear of loss as you recognize you are a deserving person. If you are romantically involved you are confident your partner will recognize and appreciate your virtues. You are confident you and your partner will enjoy a happy relationship. With self-confidence you lose your fear of rejection and loss. Jealousy is an emotion you can fully control.

The same can be said of envy. A self-confidence person will not lose time and energy wishing they had what someone else has but will decide they can get the equivalent objects for themselves through their own efforts. They do not expect to get something for nothing and do not feel badly that someone else already has for themselves what they now want. The self-confident person is happy that their friends, partner, associate, boss, neighbor, or acquaintance have desirable possessions in that it further demonstrates their value and in their eyes makes for a worthy goal for them to pursue.

So how do you improve your self-confidence thereby improving your ability to trust?

Everyone has some favorable traits. It is a good idea to make a list and to examine the list frequently. Make a list of all your good points. Perhaps a friend can help out. Are you a compassionate person? One who has empathy with the situation of others? Do you enjoy helping others? Good. That's a good start. Write that down.

Are you honest? Loyal to your friends and friend's interests? How about being dependable? Don't be modest. Write down all the good traits and characteristics you can come up with. Set the list aside for a day or two then come back to you it. You will probably be able to add a few additional items.

How about skill sets? Are you a whiz with math? How about writing skills? Do you like to read? Do you speak more than one language? Are you good with computers, iPads, iPhones, creating websites, or anything else relating to technology? Are you skilled in the use of hand tools? How about playing chess? Can you prepare delicious food? Do you sing well? Play the piano? Play the guitar? Take time to think about all the things you are good at and enjoy. Write them down. The length of the list will probably surprise you.

Put your lists in a place where they are readily in view. Study them daily and add new items as you think of them. When reviewing the list remind yourself that you already possess many desirable traits and skill sets.

Establish a series of goals for yourself. Start out by keeping the goals small and with some additional modest amount of effort doable. For example, if you are now reading one book a month push that out to two. If you only speak English but wish to also speak Spanish take action. Set a goal of speaking fluent Spanish within six months and work out a schedule so you can meet that goal.

Perhaps you like to write and for some time have been planning to write a book. Again take action. Work up your outline for the book and create a writing schedule. If you feel you can write on average one chapter a week make sure you consistently work at meeting that goal.

The goals you set should be for yourself. Do not set up a competition and don't worry about what other people are doing. Concentrate on your own accomplishments and achievements. Make sure you work on at least one of your goals every day. As you achieve your goals remind yourself that you have what it takes to be a successful person. You are a worthy human being; just look at your list of skill sets, favorable traits, accomplishments, and achievements.

Practice healthy thinking daily as you work toward meeting your goals. Make sure that over time your thinking becomes increasingly positive. You want to develop only positive thinking and drive out every bit of negativity you may have started out with. This is something that takes practice but with practice and daily reinforcement you can do it. Your positive thinking will assist you in developing self-confidence and your self-confidence will add to your positive thinking. The idea is to create a positive feedback loop so that you will be far less inclined to be envious or jealous of anyone or anything. You develop full confidence in your own abilities.

By following these simple steps you will improve your self-esteem and become a better balanced, more productive, human being and a much more desirable partner. Good luck as you consciously strive to be a better person and a better partner.

Chapter 9 – Matt and Jane

Our old friends Matt and Jane really do care for each other. Matt's jealousy caused some rough spots in their relationship. Fortunately their mutual attraction was strong enough so with effort Matt overcame his demon of jealousy. He was lucky. He was given enough time by a compassionate Jane to work on his problems.

As Matt's episodes of jealous rage and verbal abuse decreased and finally ended Jane realized she really did love the man. Since Matt worked so hard to overcome his jealous emotions and to become a compassionate and caring partner Jane was completely assured of his love. By overcoming jealousy Matt and Jane were able to stabilize their relationship on a much higher plane.

We join Matt and Jane as they have dinner in what is still their favorite restaurant.

"Are you going to order your favorite dish again?"

"You bet, Jane. I never tire of the scallops with a white wine sauce."

"Wow! Look at that. That guy by the bar looks like a runway fashion model."

"So he does, Jane. But look at the girl standing next to him. She looks like a movie star. That shirt is so short it barely covers anything. What a bod."

"Hmmmm. I didn't even see the girl. That guy is gorgeous."

"I hate to admit it but he is better looking than me. Not that is saying much."

Matt and Jane look at each other and laugh. Having a roving eye now and then is fun. There's no need to be jealous. It's natural and should be acknowledged as natural. They're happy with each other but it's still good sport to check out other people. It hasn't been easy but over the last year Matt and Jane have learned to communicate and to develop mutual respect and self-confidence that has greatly improved their relationship.

By acknowledging the presence of envy and jealousy and making a conscious effort to overcome your fears you can improve your relationships and become a happier person.

Other Books by Gerald Greene

On the Brink – War with Iran Vol. 1 -4

Force Valor Revenge

Love Lies Secrets

Surprise Bonus

Love Lies Secrets

By Gerald Greene

Love, Lies, Secrets is a work of fiction. Names, characters, places, and incidents either are the product of the author's imagination or are used fictitiously. Any resemblance to actual persons, living or dead, events, or locales is entirely coincidental. The exception is reference made to well-known public figures that are included in the book to add to the book's documentary style. Quotations attributed to public figures are entirely fictitious.

Copyright 2013 and Beyond, All Rights Reserved

Table of Contents

Chapter 1 – A Trader's Life

Chapter 2 – Jason Snow

Chapter 3 – Jason's Tale

Chapter 4 – Global Trading

Chapter 5 – Jay's Plan

Chapter 6 – Vicky Wang

Chapter 7 – Ready

Chapter 8 – Disappeared

Chapter 9 – Unwanted Secrets

Chapter 10 - NSA Asset

Chapter 11 – Secrets Secured

Chapter 1 – A Trader's Life

Hong Kong, China, 2014

Jay Steele was a lucky dude and knew it. As a recently graduated Harvard MBA yearning for adventure and fortune life in Hong Kong superseded all expectations. Shortly after graduation he turned down lucrative offers to work on Wall Street, boarded a Cathay Pacific flight to Hong Kong with one carry-on, a laptop computer, and one medium-sized suitcase and never looked back. His parents and friends thought he was crazy. That was eight years ago. Now with his new wealth they think he was smart and envied his lifestyle.

As the head foreign exchange trader for Global Trading Limited his life was like a fantasy dream. A dream come true he never wished to wake up from. By 2014 huge volatility was an ongoing feature of foreign exchange markets. Skilled traders with brass balls had the opportunity to make outrageous profits from trading operations. Jay developed into one of the best and at 31 years old was a multi- millionaire.

At six o'clock sharp he sleepily turned in bed and reached for the obnoxious noise coming from the alarm clock urging him to get ready for another tense trading day. He half way rose to hit the snooze button and then collapsed back into the bed. Just five minutes more and he would be fine. Vicky Wang, his Chinese girlfriend, rolled towards him and threw her long graceful left arm across his chest. Her shapely legs curled over his lower body. That was followed by a soft wet kiss on his left nipple.

"Hmmmm, have time for a quick one?"

"Vicky you're always tempting but I have to get moving. Can't be late today. The markets are insane. I need to be at my desk early."

"You're no fun at all. Only thinking of markets. I won't be here when you finish work. I'm flying to Honolulu this afternoon."

Yeah, I remember. I'll miss you. But seriously I have to get to work. I promise to make time for you when you return. You'll be back, when? By Friday?"

"Yup, I'll only spend one night in Honolulu and work the Friday afternoon flight to Hong Kong. You're lucky Cathay Pacific takes such good care of flight attendants. I'll have a couple of days off when I return. I'll be expecting some special time with you over the weekend."

"You'll have it. But now I have to get moving."

Jay rose from the bed and made the mistake of glancing at Vicky. She had thrown the covers off her upper body and was laying there flat on her back, hands folded behind her head, with her pert apple shaped breasts pointed towards the ceiling. She looked fantastic without makeup, even when a little unhappy. Her nipples were fully erect signaling she had not quite given up on her desire for morning activity. Vicky always slept in the nude as did Jay. Quick early morning departures were never easy. Damn, he wished he had more time.

Before heading to the bathroom to shower Jay walked over to gaze from the Kowloon harbor front floor to ceiling windows. From the seventh floor of his condominium he had an awesome view. He never tired of looking across the bustling harbor to the dynamic Hong Kong skyline. He could plainly make out the Star Ferry churning its way across the harbor to the Hong Kong side and another ferry coming toward him headed for the Kowloon dock. Across the blue green harbor the gleaming tower of The Hong Kong and Shanghai Banking Corporation headquarters building sparkled in the early morning light. Within 30 minutes Jay was seated on the Star Ferry, crossed the harbor within six minutes, and a few minutes later at his trading desk on the 88th floor of the HSBC complex. He absolutely loved the scenic commute.

Jay's trading assistant, Kathy Wong, was already in the office and brewing the first of what would be several pots of coffee consumed during the long trading day. Jay usually traded throughout the Asian market sessions and often well into the European trading day. When markets were especially active and hectic he would sometimes still be at his desk until noon or so of the North American trading day.

This meant that it was not unusual for his work day to extend towards 15 hours. He had to remain physically fit and mentally sharp to keep an edge as a top flight Forex trader. Jay religiously visited his gym three times a week to work out with his personal trainer. The trainer was a former mixed martial arts fighter who was not satisfied with Jay's work out until Jay was ready to drop. It was a great way to relieve the tension of high stakes Forex trading.

Today he took one look at his five monitors and knew that this would be one of those increasingly common extended workdays. Global markets were melting down across nearly all asset classes. Market volatility was insane and becoming even more pronounced.

"Kathy, better get ready for a doozy of a workday. The Nikkei 225 is already down over 500 points and has broken below 9,000. Dollar/Yen is following and is trading below 85.00. Japanese Prime Minster Shinzo Abe must be shitting bricks. That's not exactly what he had in mind with his drastic quantitative easing program."

Kathy brought over a freshly brewed cup of coffee. "Well, unintended consequences are the probable outcome of a fucked up global financial system. A system built upon trust doesn't function very well when no one trusts their politicians and governments. I doubt Abe will be in office much longer. Or the way things are going President Obama."

Jay looked at Kathy and smiled. What would he do without her? She was great at analyzing markets and focusing on the big picture. She could filter out the daily noise of fluctuating markets and usually determine turning points and differentiate between major and minor trends. He was the technical expert extraordinaire and expertly traded short-term moves. The proprietary computer programs he was expert with served him well. Kathy Wong was the strategic mastermind that kept the big picture in focus. Together they made a fantastic trading team.

Kathy was so smart it was scary. Educated in Hong Kong's public school system she graduated from Stanford University with a degree in mathematics and continued her education at Harvard, earning a MBA degree and ranking at the top of her class. Upon returning to Hong Kong, she moved back in with her proud Chinese parents. Jay was lucky to meet her at one of his favorite watering holes, the M Bar at the Mandarin Oriental Hotel. By chance he sat at the one vacant seat at the bar and found himself seated next to her. He immediately noticed her perfume to be subtle and intoxicating.

"Hi, there. I don't mean to intrude but I love your perfume. Mind telling me the name? If I can afford it I'd like to buy some for my girlfriend."

"No problem. It's Clive Christian No 1. And yes, it's expensive. Judging from your appearance you can afford it."

Jay did look spiffy in his new Armani suit and Hermes silk tie. In Hong Kong young men dressed for success even if they weren't successful. Jay always dressed as if he was a millionaire and due to his trading expertise actually was one several times over.

It was fantastic for a young man of 31 to be a millionaire in Hong Kong. With his trim athletic figure, jet black hair, cobalt blue eyes, TV commercial grade flashing white smile, and Black American Express card Jay gained the attention of many outrageously beautiful Hong Kong ladies. But he knew Vicky would tolerate no nonsense and didn't ever want to provoke her wrath. He deeply loved Vicky and valued the relationship. Jay was beginning to think of the one thing in life that really scared him - marriage.

While completely happy with Vicky he still enjoyed conversations with interesting Hong Kong women. He immediately was intrigued by Kathy's American English accent. Most Hong Kong ladies spoke beautiful English but with a British accent; a remnant of British colonial days. Kathy definitely spoke American English so he asked about it.

"You speak perfect English but with an American accent. Did you attend college in the United States?"

"Yes, I went to Stanford and on to Harvard for my MBA. Along the way my British accent and choice of words was corrupted by you Americans." She smiled as she said the word corrupted.

"So you're from Hong Kong? What do you do here?"

"Yes, I've lived in Hong Kong all my life except for the time I spent in America attending university. I've just returned and looking for suitable employment."

Jay perked up. He'd been looking for a trading assistant and this lady might just qualify. No problem with looks or with language. She looked lovely and sophisticated and spoke English better than he. And that perfume. The combination of looks, dress, language, educational background, and sensuous subtle fragrance was blowing him away.

"What type of work are you looking for?"

"I'm not desperate so I want something that's really a good fit. I'm quite analytical and want challenging work that will put my MBA to good use. Probably something in the financial field would interest me."

"Look, I don't want to seem too forward but I'll like you to accept my business card. I've been looking for a trading assistant to help with foreign exchange trading. How's that sound?"

"Sounds interesting. I know a little about trading Forex. My dad's always talking about exchange rates. Would I receive a bonus based upon trading desk profits? Is that a possibility?"

"You bet. My company and I like to spread the wealth. Employees seem to respond well to more money. Give me a call and we'll set up an interview at my office. I don't really like to discuss business at a bar so let's relax. No interview today. Let me buy you a drink. Is that cognac you're drinking?"

"It is. Hennessy XO if you don't mind." Kathy glanced at the business card. "I'm a little picky when it comes to cognac. Hope you don't mind Mister Steele."

"Just call me Jay. And I don't mind. You drink my favorite cognac. And your name is?'

"It's Kathy. Kathy Wong."

That was a year ago. Kathy proved to be a valuable addition to the company and worth every bit with salary and bonuses low six-figure US Dollar income. Jay's only problem with Kathy's employment was with Vicky who initially was jealous of their close working relationship. Work at the trading desk often extended well into the night beyond normal working hours. Jay was greatly relieved when after a year of employment Kathy revealed she was in a serious relationship with an American computer whiz, a Jason Snow.

"Kathy, I'm happy for you. What great news. You deserve a good man. Look I'd like to invite you and Jason to have dinner with Vicky and me. Vicky has been very curious about you. She wants to trust me but still worries about all the late nights. I'm sure she'll be pleased to learn you have a boyfriend. What about it? Will Saturday night work out?"

Chapter 2 – Jason Snow

Jay made reservations for four at the Mandarin Oriental hotel's Pierre restaurant. The Pierre was a French restaurant at a five star Hong Kong hotel and while quite expensive was one of Jay's favorites. Vicky and Jay were regulars, tipped well, and accordingly received VIP treatment. Their table had a magnificent view of the Hong Kong harbor. Even at eight o'clock at night huge cargo ships were navigating the harbor and along with lesser vessels of all descriptions left shimmering wakes illuminated by magical moonlight.

Jason Snow and Kathy appeared at the restaurant exactly at eight PM. Jay and Vicky arrived a minute later. Kathy barely had time to introduce Jason before the maître d' arrived to show them to their table.

"Mr. Steele, Miss Wang, it's so good to see you again. I've arranged for you to have a special table next to the window. From there you will have a commanding view of the harbor. I hope it's satisfactory."

"It's perfect. Mr. Yu I can always count on you. Thank you."

Jay extended his hand to offer a handshake and skillfully transferred a 50 dollar US bill into Mr. Yu's hand.

"Sir, it's my pleasure. Please let me know if you need anything. Anything at all."

The waiter, dressed in formal attire, instantly appeared. After ordering drinks all around Jay casually asked Jason how he met Kathy.

"I was very lucky. I ordered a cappuccino from a Starbucks on Connaught Road, near this hotel, and noticed this lovely lady sitting alone at the adjacent table. I couldn't take my eyes off her. Fearing she might think me a pervert or terribly rude I decided to speak up and tell her I found her very attractive. She smiled back and asked if I was visiting Hong Kong. That's how it all started."

Kathy blushed before speaking. "I normally don't speak to or encourage in any way strange men but Jason seemed pleasant enough and a bit lonely. Guess I was feeling a little lonely myself as it was Sunday and I was wondering what I should do with myself for the rest of the day. We hit it off and have been together ever since."

Vicky smiled as she told the story about meeting Jay at a Starbucks in Tokyo. "There must be something special about Starbucks. I have several friends who met their mates there."

Jason spoke up. "It must be the laid-back and civilized environment. You are actually able to have a conversation in Starbucks. That's usually not the case in a nightclub or crowded bar as the noise level is just too high. Good relationships start with good conversations. At least that's my theory."

Jay liked this guy. Jason seemed to be quite bright. He didn't dress to the standards Jay set for himself but few people had the income to play in that league. Jason wore a respectable blue blazer, an open long sleeved white shirt, and dark gray trousers. His large frame glasses and chiseled face gave him a preppy intellectual look.

Kathy told him Jason was 30 but he looked older. Probably it was his prematurely graying hair. The gray hair, green eyes, and thick glasses made him look somewhat like a geek. Jay was mature enough to know that you can't accurately judge a man by the way he dresses. Not these days. Smart business dress was expected in Hong Kong from anyone looking to advance in the business world but this was no longer the case everywhere. In America even presidents of huge public companies often favored casual dress.

"What are you doing in Hong Kong? How long have you been here?"

Jason paused for a few seconds before replying as if to decide how much information was prudent to disclose. "I've been here only three months. Can't say I'm doing much of anything except kind of hiding out. I've decided to set up an interview with a reporter from The South China Post. After that I expect life will become exciting."

"Hiding out? That sounds serious. And interviews? What about?" Jay intently focused his eyes on Jason's face. With that response to a simple question his interest in Jason soared. What was this nerdy guy into? How much did Kathy really know about this man?

"Look, we've just met so I'm not sure how much I should tell you. But what the hell, Kathy tells me you're a stand-up guy as well as the smartest guy in any room so I'll be frank with you. By the way none of this will be news to Kathy. I really appreciate her understanding and support."

"Let's order dinner first. I'm starving and Jason's tale is so interesting and yet so terrible I feel it should wait until after dinner. OK with you Jason?" Kathy looked at Jason with pleading eyes.

"Kathy, you're right. Let's relax over dinner. My story is best told with a stiff drink in hand. Anyone here speak French? I believe this menu will have to be explained to me. I hate to order mystery food."

Chapter 3 – Jason's Tale

"That was a fantastic dinner. And the wine was perfectly paired, really fabulous. Thank you." Jason looked at Jay, then Vicky, and then gazed out the window at Hong Kong harbor. Finally he turned to Kathy. "Can you stand to hear my wild tale again?"

"For sure. Tell it all. It's incredible but I believe you. The documents you've shown me are totally convincing."

Jay waited for Kathy to finish speaking, focused on Jason, leaned back in his chair and said. "My pleasure. Glad you enjoyed it. Now for an after dinner drink. And your story." Jay was very curious. Who is Jason is hiding from. The FBI? The CIA? Interpol? A former employer? A former lover? Would he tell the truth?

The waiter arrived as if by magic, four cognacs in hand. Jason proposed a toast. "May the rule of law prevail in Hong Kong."

Jay thought the toast a bit strange but said "Hear, Hear." He sipped his drink wondering what the mysterious Jason would say.

Jason began. "I was a computer freak from the time I was eight years old. My dad was an IT guy so I was encouraged to develop computer skills. Within two years my skills surpassed my dad's. By the time I entered high school I was an advanced hacker. I got into serious trouble my senior year. I foolishly decided to prove my skill set by hacking into several government websites. Even worse I hacked into computer systems used by the US military and various government agencies. I didn't mean any harm. I just wanted to see if I could do it."

"Wow! You must be a real geek. A reckless one. Of course I've heard of skilled hackers but never met one." Jason quickly began to wonder how such skills could be used to give him an edge in foreign exchange trading.

"Yeah, I thought I was a hotshot. So skilled I would never be caught. But I made the mistake of hacking into a National Security Agency (NSA) computer and before you know it there were five FBI agents swarming into the house. My poor parents were terrified. I'll never forget the look on their faces as their only child was handcuffed and led out of the house to be stuffed in the back seat of a big black SUV. I was only 17 years old."

"Shit man. That's heavy." Jay looked at Vicky. She looked stunned. She was staring at Jason as if he was dangerous. Like he was an alien from another planet.

"After hours of relentless interrogation that included many real time demos of hacking skills I was offered two choices. They could throw the book at me and I'd probably go to jail for 10 years or more or I could accept a job working for NSA. It seems they were looking for top flight hackers and were willing to make it worth their time. I was offered a starting salary of $85,000 a year. That sounded much better than residence in a juvenile detention home until I was 18 and then off to jail."

"No way! You're 17 years old, haven't even graduated from high school, and you're offered $85,000 a year by a US government agency dealing in national security?" Jay was flabbergasted. Could Jason be telling the truth? If so his hacking skills must be off the charts.

"I know it seems wild and crazy but I swear it's the truth. But hold on. My story is about to get crazier."

Kathy chimed in. "The really sad part is yet to come. At first I didn't believe Jason but he showed me documents that support his story. Let him finish."

"I worked for NSA for over 12 years. Early on I was granted top-secret security clearance. They were so pleased with my hacking ability my salary increased to $200,000 a year. I know that's not much to a successful superstar foreign exchange trader like you but to a kid who never finished high school or attended college that's not so bad. I was in hacker's haven. I was furnished with the most sophisticated computer equipment imaginable and told to commit hacking operations that became increasingly illegal all in the good name of supporting national security. I became a criminal but considered myself and more importantly by NSA a hero. I was treated well for doing my little part to keep America safe."

"Jesus Christ man. What type of information were you after?" Jay drained his glass and motioned for the waiter to bring another round.

"At first everything I was asked to do seemed to be fair game. As stated on the NSA website "The NSA/CSS core missions are to protect U.S. national security systems and to produce foreign signals intelligence information." I was tasked with hacking in to foreign computers and to extract information that would be useful to our intelligence efforts. That was a fun and challenging job. I thought I was doing a valuable service for my country."

Jay looked thoughtful as he said. "So all your work was with foreign computers?"

"Yes, for the first several years. I was really happy at NSA. But as so often happens with government agencies mission creep began. Some genius had a grand idea. Instead of seeking out and hacking into individual computers why not hack into ISP servers, Internet hubs and routers? That way we can spy on millions of individual computers. They were correct. It was a much more efficient way of collecting data."

Vicky frowned, her pert well shaped nose wrinkling in disgust. "So you think spying on foreigners is okay? Were you spying on computers in Hong Kong?"

"Nearly all governments of developed countries do it. Even when they consider the country they are spying on as a friend. You know things are always changing in the world. Look at Japan. 70 years ago they were a bitter enemy. Now they're one of our strongest allies. The same goes for Germany. Keeping up with friend and foe is vital for national security. I have no problem with that. So yes, NSA was probably collecting data from Hong Kong computers. No doubt they had a strong interest in China and were actively hacking into Chinese government and military computers. The United States has a complex relationship with China. We can't decide if they are more foe than friend."

Jay took Vicky's hand. She was visibly upset at the thought of being spied on. "So you had no problem with the NSA surveillance program?"

"No, they were doing what congress authorized them to do. What we were doing may have been considered immoral by some but under US law it was authorized by Congress and perfectly legal. I began to become uncomfortable when mission creep and the fallout from 9/11 led to the surveillance of United States citizens residing within the United States. Spying on Americans living in America without search warrants and probable cause was clearly not within NSA's legal authority."

"Whoa. You're telling me that NSA spying activity morphed into casting a wide net and spying on Americans in an indiscriminate manner?" A look of disbelief distorted Jay's face.

"I'm telling you it's worse than you can imagine. Now NSA has the ability to monitor, store, and data mine every phone conversation, every email, every financial transaction, every TV program watched, and every personnel file on every American ever living in the good old USA or anywhere in the world. Contrary to government assurances there will be no rolling back of the program. A new NSA center in Bluffdale, Utah will host supercomputers to store huge quantities of data from emails, phone calls and web searches. The $1.7bn facility is probably now operational and will contain supercomputers to store gargantuan quantities of data. Even your Google searches will be recorded. The entire life of all Americans will be permanently stored."

"My God, man. You're thinking of going to The South China Post and revealing this information in an interview? Don't do it. Your life will be turned upside down. The US government will never forgive you. You'll be branded a traitor and hunted down. Many nasty things will be said about you. You might even be disappeared."

"Yes. I'm aware of that. That's why three months ago I left NSA on good terms. I told my boss I had some urgent medical problems and had to take time off for treatment and recuperation. I came to Hong Kong three months ago and have taken my time to decide on a course of action. Once I go public I'm sure every effort will be made to discredit me, to brand me as a trouble maker, a traitor, a double agent, perhaps to make me disappear. But I've made up my mind. I have to do it. Americans have the right to know how invasive their government's spying operations are. Then they can decide if it's proper conduct by a government that's supposed to be a democratic republic."

Vicky spoke up, her beautiful Chinese face distorted and animated like a cartoon character. "I just don't get it. You're throwing a sweet life away for what? To be a despised whistleblower. What's in it for you?"

"I still have confidence in the American people. I'm willing to take the risk of being first to blow the whistle. Once my story goes public I believe other NSA employees will step forward. NSA is engaged in illegal criminal activity. I have a duty to report it. It's something I have to do even though I realize many people will brand me as a traitor rather than a patriot. I expect most of our puppet Congressman will be livid with rage and call for my immediate persecution as a traitor. You can be sure the stronger the protests the more accurate my information."

"You must know that Hong Kong has an extradition treaty with the US. Once you go public I don't think you're safe here. I can understand your attraction to Hong Kong. It's a fabulous city and Kathy is a remarkable young woman. But I believe you would be much safer in Iceland, Ecuador, perhaps even New Zealand." Jay still wondered if he was hearing the entire story. There must be many nations that would pay dearly for information Jason says he has access to.

"I have confidence in Hong Kong's rule of law. I realize that extradition is a possibility but it would be after a long legal fight and the United States probably wouldn't want the close scrutiny about NSA spying operations that would come to light in a courtroom. My greatest fears are that a rendition or assassination team is assigned to my case. That's why I've decided to go public in a major way. If I can stay in the news it will be harder for me to suddenly disappear without thorough investigations taking place. The US administration wouldn't like the findings of an independent special prosecutor investigation."

"What was the tipping point? What was the final straw that made you decide to go public?" Jay watched Jason's every gesture. Saying he wanted to bring the issue to American's attention sounded genuine but some event must have pushed him over the edge.

"It was two things. While campaigning for office President Obama promised to bring more transparency and fewer secrets to government. Once elected that promise was quickly forgotten. Obama's administration has operated under greater secrecy and prosecuted more whistleblowers than any administration in US history. I hate hypocrisy."

Jay became visibly upset as he spoke "Yes, as an American expatriate my Chinese friends question me why outright criminals in the financial community escape prosecution and under the Obama administration whistleblowers, Americans hoping to bring lies and improper acts to light, are vigorously prosecuted. Leaks of any sort are not tolerated by the Obama administration. Not even when they point out an obvious violation of duty and law. I share your disappointment with our government."

"Jay I'm glad you understand. The second reason I'm going public is I'm tired of highly placed officials lying to the America public. James R. Clapper Jr., Director of National Intelligence (DNI), recently was forced to admit that his previous statement to Congress that the NSA did not collect records on millions of Americans was a lie. Of course, he said he misspoke. The word lie is seldom used in in Washington, D.C., the domain of professional liars. I wish a pox upon them all."

Jay took a business card from his wallet and pushed it across the table. "For your sake I hope going public in a highly visible way will give you protection. Certainly, it's going to cause embarrassment for the Obama administration. I'm not sure they will want to wash that dirty laundry in public. I've found what you say fascinating as well as disturbing. I'd like to hear more details but here is not the time or place. I see the ladies are becoming upset. Let's not spoil the evening. Call me Monday afternoon and we'll set up a meeting for next week. That's cool with you?"

Chapter 4 – Global Trading

As the chief foreign exchange trader for Global Trading Limited, a Chinese company run along the lines of what in the West would be called a family business, Jay had more than an employee relationship with the principal owners. His ability to speak Mandarin at an advanced level and superior trading skills endeared him to the company's owners. He was treated as family and called "uncle" by his boss's children. Jay became what older senior Chinese business executives would call a Tai-pan. It was a status he greatly valued and would strive to keep at all costs.

The company's chairman and principal owner was Yuan Shikai, a Chinese billionaire who made his fortune in the shipping industry. The company traded personal money provided by Yuan Shikai and various extended family members as well as funds provided by a few wealthy close friends. The company's operations were not in the same league as large hedge funds but were respectable with funding in the tens of billions of dollars.

Global Trading operated with a small staff of 25 people divided into five groups involving stocks, bonds, commercial loans, real estate, and foreign exchange. As chief foreign exchange trader Jay supervised two assistant traders as well as Kathy Wong, his personal assistant and strategist. It was a small company but due primarily to Jay's skill as a Forex trader over the seven years that Jay worked for the company the return on money invested averaged in excess of 30 percent per year. With that record of success Jay was treated very well by his Chinese "family".

On Tuesday morning Jay turned to Kathy as the Yen strengthened to 85.00 against the US dollar. "Your analysis remains spot on. Dollar/Yen is trading down in lockstep with the collapsing Nikkei 225. It is ironic. As the Japanese stock market collapses and their economy remains mired in strong deflationary environment investors are rushing for the perceived safety of the Yen rather than stay in US dollars or Euros. For now it's risk off. The unwinding of carry trades is just enormous. Talk about unintended consequences. Prime Minister Abe must be wondering how much longer he'll remain in office. His efforts to inflate the Japanese economy have been a disaster."

"Let's just keep doing the hardest thing in foreign exchange trading. Let's ride the winner and see where it takes us." She burst into a wide gorgeous smile while clapping her hands in glee. This was quite a demonstration for Kathy who usually maintained a poker face around the trading desk. However, having recommended buying Yen and building a position since it broke through 98.00 she had a right to be happy. Their profits and related bonus would be enormous.

"I've scheduled a meeting with Jason Snow for three o'clock Thursday afternoon. Would you like to sit in?"

"Thanks for asking but I no longer feel comfortable around that man. I've decided to break up with him. If what he says is true and he has that interview he will soon be tailed by the FBI or CIA or who knows who. I'm not even an American and his story of NSA invasive spying on American citizens gives me the creeps. At first I applauded his bravery but now after carefully thinking it over I'm certain it's dangerous to be anywhere near him. I really like him, I sincerely do, but I see no future there. And you know how I feel about wasting time."

"Kathy, I'm surprised but do understand. At dinner Saturday you seemed so supportive. Your support actually made me nervous. I agree with you. It could be dangerous to be close to him. Vicky feels the same way. But I have something in mind that would give us a powerful trading edge if it works out."

"Jay you must be crazy. We're doing well as it is. Why risk dealing with this man? Even to be seen with him might get you on a CIA or FBI surveillance list. Hell, we don't really know how he left the NSA. We might already be on that list. I for one don't want to mess around with the US government. I'm happy as a camel on hump day and love my life in Hong Kong. I don't want to risk being disappeared."

"No problem Kathy. If I see his face or story on the front page of The South China Post I won't go near the man. I don't want to involve the company in any way. I'm not meeting him at the office. I asked you because I thought you were still his girlfriend and would want to sit in. But I have to tell you. I'm glad you've decided to break up. He seems to be a good guy with noble intentions. But the record of whistleblowers against the US government is not a good one. Whistleblowers usually end up in the scrap heap of history and their government rolls on as if they never existed."

"Well then, why risk meeting with Jason?"

"I could tell you but after thinking about it I've decided the less you know the better off you are. As Jason's ex- girlfriend, even if the relationship was for a short time, you might be interrogated someday."

"Yikes! I've learned my lesson about talking to strange lonely men at Starbucks. I'm only 25. I have plenty of time to find a mate. Being single isn't terrible, especially when thanks to you being smart enough to hire me I'm making big money bonuses on top of a generous salary. For sure,

I've decided not to risk my sweet ass over some American whistleblower computer geek."

"I don't blame you. With your income you can afford to hang out at expensive places and work at building relationships with wealthy men. Not that you're a gold digger, you already have the gold. In your situation it would be foolish to settle for some average guy. Hell girl, if you crave only occasional excitement you can afford a high class gigolo."

"Jay, you are crazy. If I ever want action I certainly don't have to pay for it. If I want I can choose between plenty of interesting good looking high income expatriate men in Hong Kong. But honestly, after working 12 to 15 hours a day who has time to play? On weekends I just want to do a little shopping and catch up on my sleep. And I mean sleep alone. Thanks to you and Global Trading my social life is just about non-existent. But I'm not complaining. I love what I do. The work is challenging and the money is exciting."

"I'm glad. We make a formidable team. After a few more years we can retire while we're still young and can enjoy traveling about the world, writing books, or whatever we choose to do. Screw the idea of working until you're an old dried up person and ready to drop."

"Hear, hear, boss man. You've got it all figured out. Now don't mess everything up by getting involved with Jason Snow. I don't like the idea of you meeting with him again. Once he goes public all hell will break loose."

Chapter 5 – Jay's Plan

Jay loved the Lobby Bar at the Intercontinental Hong Kong hotel. Located at 18 Salisbury Road, Tsimshatsui East, Tsim Sha Tsui, the hotel was close to his Kowloon home. The view across the harbor to the Hong Kong skyline was spectacular. Jay arrived at three p.m. and saw Jason sitting at a table near the floor to ceiling plate glass window. He was staring at the harbor view and appeared to be in deep thought. Before approaching the table Jay scanned the expansive lobby. Only two other tables were occupied. The tables were both occupied by elderly couples who certainly had the look of tourists. It didn't look like Jason was being followed.

"Hi Jason, been waiting long?"

"Hello Jay. No, I've just arrived. Love the view from here. It's really exciting."

"So it is. But let's get right to it. We have a measure of privacy now. But the lobby will soon fill as tourists wander in from touring about Hong Kong."

"Sure, what do you have in mind?"

"That depends. When do you have your interview?"

"Next week. Wednesday afternoon I'm scheduled to meet with one of the financial editors at The South China Post. I expect he'll call in one or two of his top reporters."

"No doubt your story will make big news. It'll be picked up by every main media outlet worldwide. You'll be famous."

"Yeah, or infamous, probably both. But I hope you're right. Being in the news in a major way will give me some protection."

I'll be completely frank with you. Once you've gone public I won't want any direct contact. If we agree to work together some secret arrangements will have to be made."

"Perfectly OK and understandable. Anyone in contact will probably be investigated. Now what do you have in mind?"

"Do you think you can hack into US Federal Reserve Bank and Department of Labor websites?"

"Wow! You're my kind of guy. Striking at the heart of Big Brother." Jason looked amused then turned poker faced and asked. "Are you serious? If I can get in how would you benefit?"

"You're a smart guy .You probably know for financial markets the US Unemployment Report is the most eagerly awaited report of the month. That's released by the Department of Labor at exactly 8:30 A.M. on the first Friday of every month. Having access to the details of that report a few minutes early would g ve me a tremendous trading edge in trading foreign exchange."

"Hmmmmm. And having access to Federal Reserve Bank data would ice that cake. Got it."

"Yeah, having early access to FOMC minutes would be helpful. The FOMC, or Federal Open Market Committee, conducts eight regular meetings every calendar year."

"Hmmmmmm. Well, based on fairly recent experience of hacking into government websites getting into the Department of Labor website is probably doable. The Federal Reserve Bank website would probably be much tougher. The government must worry that skilled hackers are drooling over the possibility of transferring a few trillion dollars in computer money to their own accounts. Heck, if hackers could transfer a few billion dollars that would probably satisfy them. By today's standards that amount of small change would probably not even be missed."

Jason was smiling but the gleam in his eyes told Jay he was interested. "I expect the security at that website is robust. That doesn't mean I couldn't get in but it's likely much more difficult and would involve far more risk of detection."

"OK, let's start with the Department of Labor unemployment report and see how it goes. I'm prepared to pay you $78,000 HK dollars per report provided the information is received at least five minutes prior to the release time. That's slightly more than 10,000 US dollars."

"Let's just make it an even 10,000 US dollars. I may not stay in Hong Kong much longer. But don't worry. For that kind of money I'll stay motivated."

"Agreed. Now how should we proceed?"

"Since you want to have no direct contact I'll have to set up a secure secret method of providing you with the data. Assuming of course I can access your requested information. Let's assume I can."

OK, you have the data. How can you safely and securely get it to me?"

"I need to purchase a new high end laptop computer for you. About 20000 HK dollars should do it."

"No problem. I'll give it to you now."

"Damn man. You are a wealthy bastard. You carry that much money around with you?"

"At times. When I think I might need it. Like today."

"I like your style. Give me a couple of days to buy the computer and set it up. I'll need to install super-duper encryption software as well as software that will completely hide your IP address. I'll use a series of proxy servers that will make you appear to be operating from the moon. On second thought maybe just for fun I'll make it appear that you're accessing the Internet from Moscow. The Kremlin is a good Moscow Internet address." Jason chuckled as he visualized the confusion of anyone trying to trace the pimped out computer.

"I'll have to build a special website for you. What would interest you? A good porn site, an adventure travel site, a current news site, anything at all? Your wish is my command."

"How will this work?"

"It's easy. Once my software is installed you'll be able to access the website without revealing your true IP address. Actually, you'll be able to anonymously surf anywhere about the Internet. You can visit your favorite porn sites and no one will ever know.

Using encryption software you'll log into your website, I'll have it bookmarked for you. Once logged in, as if by magic. You'll be on a secret page where your requested data will be posted. That's it. Simple, assuming I can hack into the Department of Labor website without being detected and steal the unemployment report release. Now what type of website do you want as your visible site? I'll pick out a snazzy domain name for you and camouflage ownership."

"Let's go with the adventure travel site. Adventure travel always appealed to me. How long will this take?"

"Your computer and website will be ready in a couple of days. I don't know how long it will take to hack the Department of Labor website. I'll give it a go right away and let you know. Let's meet again next Monday at the same time and place. 'll give you your computer and report on my progress. Is that okay? Oh. one more thing. Payment."

"I didn't think you would forget that small matter."

"It may be small to you but remember I'm recently unemployed. I could sale my information to wil ing governments for a fortune but I don't want to do that. So here's the deal. When you log into your new website you'll find a link to an invoice page. Follow the instructions on that page. You'll wire the money to my consulting company for services rendered. You can print out the invoice for your own records. Whenever possible I like to keep things simple."

"Perfect. Let's have one more drink. I promised Vicky I wouldn't be late tonight. She told me this morning she has something she wants to show me."

Chapter 6 – Vicky Wang

Vicky Wang grew up in Hong Kong. Her parents relocated from Shanghai, China when she was barely three to seek a life offering more opportunity. They soon opened a modest seafood restaurant and through years of hard work and sacrifice expanded their business to include a small chain of seven seafood restaurants spread across Hong Kong. As an only child Vicky greatly benefited as her parents overcame their humble beginnings and became well to do upper middle class Hong Kong citizens.

She was showered with love and affection while being taught to work hard and to always do her best. Like most hard-working Chinese parents they placed a high value on education and pushed Vicky to excel in school. Vicky always wished to please her parents and was an excellent student. Education in Hong Kong was rigorous and largely modeled on that of the English system. English was taught as the international language of business along with Cantonese and Mandarin. Vicky became fluent in all three languages and while attending college added Japanese to the mix.

"Vicky this is what you want? You're sure? With your grades any college would be glad to have you."

"Daddy, I'm sure. A degree from The School of Hotel and Tourism Management will open a lot of doors. I enjoy working with people, have good social skills, and the tourism industry is big business in Hong Kong."

That discussion took place nine years ago. A few weeks before graduating with a degree in hotel management Vicky answered an ad placed by Cathay Pacific Airlines. Like many women born in Shanghai to families with deep roots in that northern Chinese city she was tall and however dressed cut an elegant figure. Her good looks, charm, poise, language ability, and friendly nature impressed the interview team. She was placed on the short list of qualified applicants. After waiting a nervous six weeks Vicky received a letter from Cathay Pacific offering a position as a flight attendant trainee provided she presented her degree and passed an intensive physical examination.

After three years of hard work in economy and business class Vicky was promoted to work in the First Class cabin. On a trip from Hong Kong to Tokyo she met Jay at a Starbucks at Haneda Airport. After a quick shopping excursion with a girlfriend in the Ginza District she was on her way to returning to duty when a Starbucks latte became a must have item.

Jay was single with a weakness for Starbucks coffee and good looking Chinese women. "Excuse me Miss. Weren't you working this morning as a flight attendant on the Cathay Pacific Hong Kong to Tokyo flight?"

"Yes Sir I was. Were you on the flight?"

"I was. I had a meeting with clients this afternoon and took the early flight from Hong Kong. I believe you served me breakfast."

"Sorry Sir. I don't remember. We are pretty rushed on that flight. "

"I'm sure it was you. It's quite a coincidence meeting you here."

"Yes Sir. It certainly was. Nice talking to you but my girlfriend and I must be going. We're working the 8:10 P.M. flight to Hong Kong and have to report for duty."

"I can't believe it. I'll be on that flight. Perhaps you'll serve me dinner." Jay took another long look at Vicky and decided to introduce himself.

"My name is Jay Steele. I'm really glad to see you again."

"I'm Vicky Wang. See you on the flight." Vicky revealed a dazzling smile, finished her latte with one sip, and hurriedly walked out of Starbucks. Jay watched her every sensuous swaying step. He knew he was acting like a juvenile fool but was smitten. That's how it all began.

Before Jay met Jason Snow he and Vicky had been living together for 18 months. From that chance meeting in Tokyo a love story quickly developed. Vicky's fellow flight attendant shopping girlfriend was shocked and a little jealous as their relationship developed. No one should be that lucky, not even her best friend.

Jay hastily finished his drink, confirmed he and Jason would meet again the coming Monday, said goodbye, and started to walk out of the hotel. He walked by a gift shop. Remembering Vicky wanted to show him something that evening he decided to reciprocate and purchase a gift.

"What do you have in gold necklaces? Nothing too large or fancy. My girlfriend's neck is delicate so a simple chain will do fine. Any ideas?"

The shopkeeper was an elderly Chinese man with a well-trimmed white beard and mustache. He wore a dark blue bow tie with white polka dots and a gray herringbone jacket which gave him a knowledgeable, distinguished, dignified appearance. Without hesitation he replied. "I have just the necklace Sir. Let me show you."

He unlocked the showcase and placed a fine woven gold necklace on a purple velvet cloth spread across the counter. The shopkeeper must be a mind reader. Jay thought it perfect and visualized fastening it around Vicky's neck. He knew she would be pleased.

"Vicky I'm home."

A musical voice answered from the kitchen. "Hi Jay, I can't believe it. You remembered not to be late. Come here. I want to show you something."

Jay stepped in the kitchen to see a five foot eight shapely Chinese girl with long black hair tapering down to the small of her back dressed only in bra and panties. She'd been preparing dinner but turned to give Jay a full frontal view.

"On my last trip to Honolulu, Joy, Noi, and I decided to check out a few shops on Kalakaua Avenue. I found these sweet items at Victoria's Secret.

How do you like them?" Vicky flashed her devastating smile as she asked the question with the all too obvious answer.

"I love them. Is that what is called a Bombshell Bra? Your boobs are lovely and at least two cups larger than I remember. They're desperately trying to escape from that bra. Please understand I'm not complaining. You look fantastic."

"Only fantastic? I was hoping for more of a reaction than that."

"I'm not a good enough wordsmith to come up with a better word. But there's nothing wrong with my reaction. See for yourself."

Vicky glanced at his crotch and giggled. "I see what you mean. Well, what are you going to do about it?"

Jay swooped to Vicky's side and picked her up in his muscular arms. His trips to the gym were paying off. As he headed for the bedroom with his precious cargo he remembered his gift. That could wait. As could dinner. At the moment there were more important tasks to perform.

Later that evening Jay presented Vicky with the gold necklace. She slightly turned her head and extended her neck. Jay moved behind her, brushed her hair to the side, and fastened the necklace just as he had visualized at the gift shop. "I love you Vicky Wang. Truly I do."

"And I love you Jay Steele. And always will. Now what are we going to do about it?"

"I don't want to lose you. Not now. Not ever. It's my fear of changing the relationship that scares me. So many married couples start out great and end up divorced. Something seems to change. Love turns to hate. That scares me."

"That's true. But other couples make it work and their relationship only improves with time. My parents are a good example. They've worked together, struggled together, and helped each other, for over 30 years and their marriage is better than ever. I believe we can do that. I'd like to see us try."

Vicky let me get beyond this deal I'm working on. Then let's take a vacation and talk this completely out. I'm crazy about you. I just need a little time to relax, clear my head and overcome my fear. Fair enough?

"OK Jay. Just remember I won't wait forever. I want to be an honest woman, have kids, and then grow old with the man I love. And please. If you're planning any sort of deal with Jason Snow don't do it. I have bad vibes about having anything to do with that man. If he'll betray his country he's capable of betraying anyone. Please don't get involved with him."

Chapter 7 – Ready

On Monday Jason was a few minutes late arriving at the Lobby Bar at the Intercontinental Hong Kong Hotel. It had been a hectic day with the Yen selling off during Asian trading hours before heading his way as European markets opened. Jason was seated at the same table in the same seat as their last meeting. Once again he seemed to be in deep thought as he stared through the huge floor to ceiling window across the always bustling harbor. A new Apple laptop computer was next to a briefcase and rested on the table.

"Hi there Jason. Sorry to keep you waiting. Have you been here long?"

"No, I've just arrived. How are you?"

"I'm great. How about a gin and tonic? It's awfully warm today."

"Not for me, thanks. You probably noticed I brought you a laptop computer along with a briefcase. In the briefcase you'll find written instructions. My advice is to memorize them, then burn the documents.

"All right, I'll do that. Are you sure about a drink?"

"Jay, I must be getting paranoid. I haven't gone public with my whistleblowing yet feel uncomfortable in public places. Rather than sit here and drink I'd rather just go. You should leave a few minutes later carrying the computer. In the instructions you will see how we can secretly stay in touch. Remember my interview with The South China Post reporter is this Wednesday. I'm sure the shit will start hitting the fan within a few hours after the paper runs the story.

"How will I know if your hacking is successful?"

"Everything is explained in the instructions. It's simple."

OK, then. Good luck to you."

"Thanks. And good luck with your trading." Jason rose, offered his hand in a firm businesslike handshake, and headed toward the main exit. Thursday morning Jay saw his photo on the front page of The South China Post and on CNN International.

"Waiter, gin and tonic please." Jay resisted the urge to read the documents in the briefcase. Instead he placed the computer in the case, closed the latch, had one drink, and headed home.

Jay was glad Vicky was on a flight to Beijing, China. He could read the documents in complete privacy. The instructions on receiving data were simple. Once logged in using the encryption software if meaningful data was posted he would see the word "ready" in bold red print. All he had to do was follow the link. Another clickable link was for messages. The number of unread messages would be highlighted. That was it. As Jason said, simple. The special software did all the work of keeping things private.

Jay was alarmed at the contents of some of the documents stuffed into the briefcase with the computer. Along with his operating instructions there was a copy of a letter from President Obama to Attorney General Eric Holder authorizing the use of wiretaps and other invasive spying devices on any American suspected of being involved with terrorism. The authorization did not mention probable cause or the need to obtain court orders or warrants.

There were copies of other documents demanding that Verizon, AT&T, Sprint, and other Internet and telecommunications companies make data available to the government covering telephone conversations, and use of the Internet including emails, downloads, and surfing. The commands were such so that no American citizen was exempt from government intrusion and outright spying. Jason was not pleased to have these documents in his possession. He realized the danger of having documents classified as top secret in his hands but didn't want to destroy such important documents. He was outraged that the government seemed to willfully disregard the rights of Americans. Jason must be telling the truth.

As Jason forecast all hell broke loose Thursday morning. Jason's picture was on the front page of the newspaper and a lengthy article made the case that the NSA, FBI, and CIA were routinely spying on Americans living in America and elsewhere. According to the article the agencies were casting a wide net and disregarding the legal requirement of obtaining court orders or even having probable cause. The story was picked up by the major wire services and TV channels and blasted all over the world.

Kathy, usually a cool steady hand, was agitated. "Jay have you seen this morning's paper? The story is already on CNN. I'm glad I broke off with that guy. I'll never talk to a strange man at Starbucks again. I swear."

"That guy wasn't kidding around. I guess he really did work for NSA."

"It's so terrible. All of it. The US government spies on American citizens and the world. Then a NSA employee goes public with classified top secret information. It's all bad in my opinion." Kathy was as upset as Jay had ever seen her.

"I'm sure it will get worse. Jason prophesized the Washington outpouring of rage and condemnation of his actions would be intense. He knew he would be cast as a traitor and a no good ungrateful villain. Some of the attacks would be funny if the issue weren't so serious. One Senator portrayed Jason as a high school dropout who has a history of personal problems and a complete failure at everything he ever tried. If true the old fool didn't consider what that means for NSA hiring practices. I can't really believe the agency would give top secret clearance and pay $200,000 a year to someone they considered a complete screw-up flunky."

"Your right, even a Hong Kong girl knows NSA doesn't hire fools. Formal education or not Jason is brilliant. And articulate. I do wonder about his judgment. I don't see a sound exit strategy. In Hong Kong whistle blowers usually don't fare well. I expect the same is true for America. Coming to Hong Kong seeking safety seems risky to me." Kathy shifted focus back to her monitor and broke into a wide smile. "At least our Yen trade is ignoring the news. Go Yen baby go. I want to vacation in Bali this year."

It was one week until the unemployment report and Jay hadn't heard from Jason. He wondered if Jason was able to hack into the Department of Labor computers. Every day he would log into his special webpage. No messages so far. Nothing at all.

Finally at 8:00 P.M. on the first Friday of the month a "ready" message was posted. It was 8:00 A.M. in Washington and the report would be released in 30 minutes. Jay took one look at the data.

"Kathy trade large. Sell 100 Million US Dollar/Yen at market."

"What! So close to the report?"

"You bet. I've got a strong feeling the report will knock the socks off the Dollar. We'll be quick to cover and bank a few hundred thousand to cap off our week." The market expected the unemployment rate to remain the same at 7.8% and the non-farm payroll jobs to be at 165,000. Jason's "ready" information put the rate at 8.0% and the payroll at 115,000. If correct that was a big miss and should send the Dollar sharply lower; at least for the first few minutes after the release.

"Ok, boss. We're in there. 50 mil at Citibank and 50 at Chase. Hope you're right. "

"Me too. Be ready to cover. On this trade we won't stick around long. We'll let our long term positions ride."

Jay was usually cool as a cucumber while at the trading desk. But at 8:29 he was sweating profusely. Even worse he desperately needed to pee. There was no time now. He would have to squirm in his seat and tough it out. There it was. At 8:30 EST, over the Thomson Reuters dealing trading service news feed, the unemployment report data matched up perfectly with the data posted on his website's secret communication page.

Before the release the Dollar had rallied slightly against the Yen and the position was at a $50,000 loss. At 8:31 the position moved favorably to a $150,000 profit. The Dollar/Yen chart showed a green line moving straight down the chart. Beautiful. As the Yen strength accelerated the profit ballooned to $525,000. There was a moment of hesitation; the profit backed up to $415,000. Jay grew tense before Yen strength kicked in again and accelerated. At 8:41 the profit reached $980,000.

"Cover! That's good enough. Let's not be greedy."

Kathy was lightning fast with the dealing service. Faster than Jay. "Done, boss. Wahooo! That's a good eleven minutes work. Your hunch was spot on."

Within seconds of Jay's order to cover Yen began to give up some of its gain as a round of Dollar/Yen short covering hit the market. As usual Jay's timing was immaculate. He earned $980,000 for the company of which 20 percent would go into his bonus pool. Out of that $196,000 he would pay

Kathy 10 percent or $19,600 leaving him a decent potential bonus of $176,400. Of course, as the bonus was paid annually he had to maintain profits within the pool.

The first thing Jay did after covering the position was to walk briskly to the men's room. He was about to explode. He soon returned. A huge grin lit up his face. "Kathy, let's call it a wrap. It's been a long week. That was a great way to close it out."

"Super. I think I'll go straight home, feed my cats, and open a nice bottle of red wine. For sure I'll look through that dreamy looking brochure about vacationing in Bali. Damn, I love this job."

"It is exciting isn't it? But we need to stay cool. Tonight I was a little nervous waiting for the report. I'll have to work on that."

"I suggest you pee a few minutes beforehand. After covering our position I noticed the desperate look on your face and quick trip to the men's room."

Chapter 8 – Disappeared

The month passed by quickly. Jason Snow was all over the news but the uproar seemed to quickly die down. It seemed every official in the Obama government branded him a lousy traitor and all around flunky. Poll after poll showed the majority of the American public sided with the administration. There was a congressional investigation with the head of NSA the main witness but nothing seemed to come of it. Wide spread spying was said to be necessary to protect Americans.

It was business as usual in Washington which meant many hours of hearings. Witness after witness testified how necessary the spying programs were to national security. As a whistleblower Jason had no friends in Washington. More than 50% of Americans stated they were more than willing to give up privacy in return for assurances they would be safer from terrorism. The NSA programs moved full speed ahead.

Jay shorted a few million Euros from the 1.3410 level while maintaining his heavy position in Japanese Yen. After losing ground against the Dollar and slipping to 86.50 the major trend kicked in and Yen surged to 84.00. Poor Prime Minster Abe. His ambitious and audacious plan to reflate the Japanese economy by weakening the currency became his worst nightmare. The Japanese government bond market (JGB) collapsed as he set a two percent inflation goal and pumped up the money supply. The Nikkei 225 index moved into bear market territory. As the Nikkei plunged the Yen strengthened. Prime Minister Abe was definitely losing the currency wars.

"Weird isn't it? The unintended consequences of implementing Abe's plan are the exact opposite of what he expected. With the Fed tapering off quantitative easing the unwinding of risk on trades fueled a massive strengthening of Yen. Yen strength accelerated big time after Abe announced he was stepping down." Kathy was as much talking to herself as to Jay. Their positions had substantial life changing profits and she was beginning to think they should exit the market and relax. Something they hadn't done for a stressful long time. She was young but knew excessive greed could be a terrible thing. Markets could turn brutally fast and profits could disappear in a flash.

"Kathy, I know what you're thinking. And I agree. Let's start closing out Yen positions. 20 mil at a time. We'll still trade heavy on unemployment report day. I've got good feelings about that action."

"You and your good feelings. Better stick to reading your charts and indicators. I'd rather rely on reading tea leaves than bet on your feelings."

"Come on Kathy. Don't you ever use women's intuition and feelings to scope out markets?"

"Never. But I admit I do occasionally visit Chinese fortunetellers."

"Yikes. I wish you'd kept that tidbit of info to yourself. Well, whatever works is fine. Just a few days until a new month and the unemployment report. Start scaling down our long-term positions. Let's get ready for the report."

There wasn't any communication from Jason since the last unemployment report data was posted. Jay grew nervous as the first Friday of the month approached. Every few hours he logged into his website and checked for new data.

"What's the deal Jay? You seem as nervous as a guy thinking about getting married. Are you and Vicky finally about to take the drastic step?"

"Ask me about markets, not my personal life. Are you jealous? Can't stand the thought of my being with someone else?"

"Don't flatter yourself. You seem to be more on edge than usual, that's all. It's only July. I want to see that bonus pool continue to grow all year. If you're having a case of nerves, that's not good. You should take a vacation in August along with all the other foreign exchange trader big shots."

"I Agree. Vicky and I plan to take a two week vacation next month. She gets 21 days of vacation a year and I'm overdue for some time off so we can probably make it happen. You can help me out. We should work out of our Yen positions within a few days. Just keep covering on Yen rallies. We'll let the Euro trade run. You've done a great job so far. I'm confident you can handle things while I take a couple of weeks off."

"Thanks. I'll do my best. Being flat Yen with huge profits booked should put us more at ease. I want you to have a restful stress free vacation so you'll come back in a good mood. Then I'll ask for some time off."

"You'll have earned it. Now continue to scale out of our Yen trade as it moves below 84.00 and clear the decks for unemployment day. That'll help to improve my mood even before a vacation break."

It was the first Friday in August and still no word from Jason. With nothing posted to the webpage by 8:25 PM local time Jay decided to stand down for this report. That turned out to be prudent. An unemployment rate of 8.0 and non-farm payroll numbers of plus 155,000 was expected. The actual numbers were reported at 8.0 and 157,000. With actual numbers being so close to forecast no obvious movement of Dollar/Yen or Euros could be determined. Jay only wanted to take advantage of wide misses. Even if data had been posted to the website he would not have traded this report.

"Kathy, I'm going to call it a day. Baby sit the positions until about noon EST then lock it up. With that report it should be a boring close to the week. Be sure to have a great weekend."

"Yeah, thanks Jay. My cats and I will have a ball."

Jay wanted to go home and think things over. Was his deal with Jason to end so soon? Wonder how he's doing? And where could he be hiding out? The newspapers all report the NSA, CIA, and FBI are looking for him. It seemed strange they couldn't locate him with all the resources those agencies have in Hong Kong. On the Star Ferry while looking at the dramatic Hong Kong side skyline a terrible thought crossed Jay's mind. Perhaps Jason had been tracked down. Perhaps he already was secretly disappeared. The chilling thought made Jay shiver. Before the ferry docked fear was racing through his mind.

Chapter 9 – Unwanted Secrets

Jay was home by 9:30. Vicky rushed to meet him dressed in only loose fitting white silk pajamas.

"I'm glad you're home early. The first Friday of the month is usually your late night."

"I'm glad you're here to greet me. How was your flight to Honolulu?"

"Not bad. Not bad at all. Look, the girls and I got in a little beach time." Vicky slowly unbuttoned her pajama top to reveal distinct tan lines surrounding two inviting islands of pearly white breasts.

"So I see. That's a lot of tan and not much white. I'm not sure I like your new bikini top."

"Don't be a prude Jay. It's quite fashionable. You seem to like tiny bikinis on other girls. Don't I measure up?"

Jay realized this was a discussion he could not win so quickly changed the subject. "Please open a bottle of red wine while I change. Cabernet Sauvignon would be good. After checking one thing on my computer I'll dedicate the rest of the evening to you. How's that sound?"

"That sounds good. Don't be long."

Jay changed into a comfortable track suit. He booted up his laptop at the bedroom desk and moments later logged into his secret web page. He gasped. There was a new clickable link that said only "NSA Documents". Jason must have posted within the last hour.

"Jay, I've poured the wine. And I'm lonely." Vicky's voice sounded like it came from a million miles away. The title "NSA Documents" scared him shitless. What was Jason up to? What had he done?

"Vicky I'm really sorry but I'll be a few more minutes. Have to check something out."

"Don't be long. It's a weekend you workaholic. I don't want to spend it alone."

"Give me five minutes. I promise no more." Jay hoped that was true. Hoped there wouldn't be much to look at. Hoped Jason was only pulling his chain. He clicked the link.

"Oh shit. Jesus, what's this?' There was a message that said "read this first". It looked brief so he started reading.

"Jay, sorry to hit you with this man but you're the only person I trust to do the right thing. You know we're partners in crime. NSA or FBI or CIA agents (maybe all three) are closing in on me. I discovered agents were asking questions at my last hotel. Luckily I changed hotels yesterday but I know they're close behind. I've created PDF files of top secret NSA documents and posted them to your webpage. My copies are on a thumb drive but I must destroy it. When they find me I'm sure they'll look through everything. Thumb drives will be number one on their list. I know it's a role you don't want but now you're keeper of the secrets. Do with them as you see fit. Probably you won't see or hear from me again. Sincerely, Jason Snow

Jay's only thought was "Oh God! I was crazy to deal with America's most wanted man."

"Jay." Vicky was becoming impatient.

"I'm coming honey. Let me power down the computer." He didn't have the courage to start reading documents tonight. Jay wondered if it was a crime to have top secret stuff on his computer. Damn. He should see a good lawyer before even looking at the first document. How could he explain receiving documents without revealing his trading information scheme? He should delete them all. But he was curious. Besides no one would believe he deleted them without first taking a look. And experts could recover files even after they've been deleted.

Vicky looked unhappy. Her glass was empty. She was pouring another drink as Jay entered the entertainment room. The large flat screen TV was on and an old Bruce Lee martial arts movie starting. "I'm always waiting on you." She was sitting on the leather sofa tanned legs folded beneath her, pajama top unbuttoned, and motioned for Jay to join her. Vicky's frown turned into a welcoming smile as he sat beside her and reached for the wine glass. Before he could take the first sip she took his hand and pressed it against her breast. Vicky's pert nipples were already hard. The documents would have to wait.

Vicky looked like an angel as she slept. Last night, after finishing a second glass of wine, she was affectionate, energetic and wild. Jay quickly forgot about Jason Snow and secret documents and became lost in making love. Saturday morning Jay carefully untangled himself from Vicky's long legs and arms. He slipped out of bed, threw on his favorite track suit, and booted up the laptop. He was careful not to disturb Vicky. She had earned her beauty sleep. Besides he wanted to look at the documents in private.

Jay gasped as he saw the long line of links extending completely down the page. Each link opened to a PDF file. There were a total of 10 pages with 25 links per page. Each link was clickable text such as "President Obama to Eric Holder" and the date of the document. After following page one links and downloading 25 documents Jay had no desire to continue. The secrets contained in only 10% of the total were enough to get him killed. How in the world did Jason manage to steal such stuff from NSA?

He heard Vicky moving about the kitchen. The smell of coffee triggered an urgent desire. He wanted to join Vicky, drink coffee together, go for a nice brunch, and forget he'd ever heard of Jason Snow and the NSA. That's what he wanted. But that wouldn't help him find a way out of trouble. He had to talk to someone. That would help him figure it out. Who else but one he trusted more than anyone else?

"Vicky, let's have our coffee at the dining room table. I need to talk."

"Sure, what's up? You sound serious."

"I have good reason. There's no excuse for letting greed trump judgment but that's what I've done."

"Having problems with a trade?" Vicky looked puzzled. Jay never discussed his trades.

"No honey. All is fine with my trade positions. Actually I'm doing better than ever."

"Well then, what? I hope I can help."

"You remember Kathy's recent boyfriend, Jason Snow?"

"Sure. He's the NSA creep that's all over the news. Are they still seeing each other?

"No, she had good reason to break off. Look, I don't want to get into details. It's better if you don't know. If you're ever interrogated you can honestly say you only know I met with him a couple of times."

"Interrogated? Why should I be interrogated?"

"Jason transferred some top secret NSA files to my computer."

"What! How could he do that? And why?

"I was totally surprised. I expected business files. I guess he thought if anything happened to him I would protect them and see them made public."

"Jay, you have to report this. Having stolen top secret files on your computer must be a crime. What if Jason's activities can be traced?"

"Probably you're right. But If I report to the NSA or FBI they will surely want to examine my computer."

"So? What's wrong with that?"

"There's some other stuff that would get me in serious trouble. Maybe even a jail term."

"My God Jay! Don't tell me you have child porn on your hard drive."

"No, nothing like that. The files are business related. But illegal."

"Damn Jay. You better seek legal advice. I couldn't stand it if you went to jail. You know I'm a Hong Kong material girl. I admit I was spoiled growing up; treated like a little princess. I like nice things. I love you Jay. But I'm not the type to suffer staying home alone while her man serves a ten year prison term. My job gives me plenty of chances to get into relationships with rich attractive men. I'd never do that as long as I'm with you. But if you were locked up ---." Vicky's voice broke as she burst into tears.

"Please don't cry. I'll see my attorney. We'll figure something out." He moved to Vicky's side and softly kissed her on the forehead. His eyes couldn't focus. He felt ill, very ill.

Chapter 10 - NSA Asset

"That's the story Mr. Chan. And that's my computer. With an encryption key you can log into the website and follow links to PDF files of secret NSA documents. A lot of the stuff hasn't been released by Jason Snow. How can I be protected?"

"That's a fascinating story Mr. Steele. Scary. In newspapers and on CNN I've seen Mister Snow's accusations of the United States NSA illegally conducting widespread spying against American citizens. I knew he was in Hong Kong but never dreamed I'd get involved with the case. You've done the right thing. You need a solicitor."

"I'm sure I do. Now what can you do for me?"

"I'm confident the American government would love to have that computer and access to the website. I understand so far only a small fraction of incriminating and damaging material has been released by Mr. Snow. If your fears about his whereabouts and safety are correct he won't be releasing further information. That means you're the only remaining source that could leak secret documents. That places you in a dangerous position. By coming forward I think an indemnification deal can be worked out .You agree to turn over the computer, encryption key, and all documents. In return they agree not to prosecute no matter what they find on your hard drive and website."

"Will you negotiate for me?"

"Yes, I'll take the case if you like. I'll require a 50,000 Hong Kong dollar retainer to get started. I'll need to prepare an indemnification agreement and arrange to meet on your behalf with the Hong Kong NSA section chief. I can probably locate his whereabouts by contacting the American Consulate."

"OK, Sir. Please get started as soon as possible. I'm a nervous wreck with this hanging over my head. With my job it's not good to be overly nervous."

30 minutes later Jay enters his home. "Vicky, I'm home"

"I'm in the bedroom. Packing for another trip."'

"Where to this time? Seems you've only gotten home."

"Have a three day trip. To Beijing, Shanghai, back to Beijing, and then back to Hong Kong."

"I'll miss you."

"Ha! You're sure? I'll been home for two days and you've hardly noticed."

"Sorry Vicky. I had to print out a lot of documents. I'm finally finished. By the time you return I hope to be out of trouble. I just came from an encouraging meeting with my attorney. I guess to you that's solicitor. By the time you return we should be able to go out and celebrate."

"I hope so. You seem so worried. I want my old Jay back. Well, I have to be off. The van will pick me up any time now. I'll call you from Beijing." Vicky left in a rush. She didn't want to risk keeping the pickup van waiting.

The next afternoon Mr. Chan called Jay at his office. "Good news Mr. Steele. I met with a Mr. John Shaw, Hong Kong NSA section chief, and he's accepted the indemnification agreement. We're to meet at 10.45 tomorrow morning at the American Consulate at 26 Garden Road, Central, Hong Kong. Be sure to bring your computer. I suggest you drop by my office first and we'll go together. Make it 10:00 sharp. Is that satisfactory?"

"That's great news. I want to leave a large file of documents with you for safekeeping. They are already in a package addressed to the business editor of The South China Post. I've even put postage on the package. Please drop it in the mail should anything happen to me. Will you do that?"

"I'm sure you'll be fine, don't worry. But yes, I'll accept the package and hopefully never have to place it in the mail."

"Great. Thank you. I'll drive my car as the package is awkward to carry about. I have a new BMW 750i Sedan that's hardly been out of my parking space. See you tomorrow."

Chapter 11 – Secrets Secured

John Shaw didn't become Hong Kong NSA section chief by being a nice guy. He knew it was a tough world out there and after 27 years with the NSA knew a lot about keeping America safe. Safely for America increasingly depended upon good intelligence. To John Shaw it didn't make any difference if the NSA collected intelligence overseas by spying on foreign nationals or if intelligence was collected domestically by spying on who ever planned to hurt US interests. It mattered not at all if the perpetrators were foreign or American nationals. Anyone plotting against the United States was fair game. It didn't concern him that millions of innocent Americans might be spied on to find one person with evil intent.

He was proud of the work his agency, the CIA, and FBI had done on the Jason Snow case. As soon as the articles appeared in The South China Post Mr. Snow was charged by the US Attorney General with espionage and theft. The three agencies sprung immediately into action. The former NSA employee left the hotel he'd been saying at for nearly three months and moved into what he thought would be a safe apartment. A paid informant at the apartment complex phoned in a tip that he thought he recognized Jason Snow. The rest was easy. In the future the American government would not have to worry about Mr. Snow leaking top secret classified information. Justice was carried out swiftly and efficiently.

Under enhanced interrogation the traitor revealed he passed top secret documents to a Jay Steele. Mr. Steele was located and action was about to be taken when his attorney called requesting a meeting. Perfect. He looked forward to this morning's 10:45 appointment. The target was coming to him. He could hardly wait to get his hands on that computer.

"Has our asset arrived?" John Shaw asked special agent Bob Cooper as Cooper walked into the American consulate conference room.

"Yes Sir. He arrived in Hong Kong last night. He's been briefed and should be tailing the target as we speak."

"Good. As our meeting breaks up be sure to detain the attorney. Invite him to lunch with Consul General Young. An ambitious attorney won't turn that offer down. Explain to Mr. Steele that he shouldn't wait. Mr. Chan will be detained quite a while on official business."

"Will do. Should I give the asset the green light?"

"Wait until we have the computer in hand and check it out. We'll hold Steele here until we've done that.

The meeting was brief. Mr. Shaw seemed friendly enough and complemented Jay for his decision to turn over the computer and documents. He actually praised him for being a true patriot. Jay asked Mr. Chan if he could make his way back to his office after his business meeting with the Consulate General Assured that would not be a problem Jay left the American Consulate grounds and walked one block to the parking garage. He felt a great sense of relief. He was back.

His car was packed on the top deck of a five story parking garage. Jay unlocked the BMW, fastened the seat belt, sat still for a moment enjoying the new car smell of leather seats, and then pushed the ignition button.

A tremendous boom reverberated throughout Central Hong Kong. From the top deck of the parking garage angry black smoke plumes laced with reddish orange fingers billowed sixty feet into the hot shimmering summer sky. A couple walking to their vehicle three parking spaces away were knocked to the concrete deck by the blast. Multiple shrapnel wounds disfigured their burned bodies. The blast shockwave rattled thick blast proof American Consulate windows.

John Shaw had both hands on one of the conference room window panes. His eyes followed the thick toxic smoke as it rose into the sky. He slightly smiled as he turned and spoke to agent Bob Cooper. "Once again NSA wins. America's secrets are secure."

Recommended Reading

Envy

Inferno

Gerald Greene Author Page

www.ingramcontent.com/pod-product-compliance
Lightning Source LLC
Chambersburg PA
CBHW071313060426
42444CB00034B/2207